IMPROVING INTELLIGENCE INTEGRATION AMONGST
THE INTELLIGENCE COMMUNITY

ABSTRACT

IMPROVING INTELLIGENCE INTEGRATION AMONGST THE INTELLIGENCE COMMUNITY, by Major Michael D. Norton, 57 pages.

Gathering and sharing intelligence is crucial to ensuring our national security. The intelligence community (IC) is commonly blamed when there is a failure to foresee actions against U.S. interests at home and abroad. While intelligence is usually compartmentalized, there are occasions where the benefits of sharing intelligence far outweigh the risks. The author believes intelligence sharing amongst members of the community has increased since the Intelligence Reform and Terrorism Prevention Act of 2004 (IRTPA), however the overall effectiveness of that sharing leaves much room for improvement.

Members of the IC habitually keep information from each other in the name of secrecy and because of differing missions and personnel security procedures. This thesis seeks to identify the ways in which the sharing of information between the members of the IC has improved since the IRTPA of 2004. The author will describe the composition of the IC and how it was aligned prior to the reform as well as today. The author reviews recommendations that were made prior to the reform and identifies why those recommendations were not implemented. The author also summarizes the details of the reform and the changes made by IRTPA.

ACKNOWLEDGMENTS

To complete a Master of Military Arts and Sciences degree takes commitment that is indicative of a professional military officer. It is this commitment that enabled the author to volunteer for the project and devote the past year to researching, analyzing, and ultimately providing recommendations that one day may in fact improve the way the members of the Intelligence Community operate. There are many people that made this possible and they deserve much more than a simple thank you.

First, I would be remiss if I did not thank my thesis committee. While the author tried hard not to bother the committee as much as possible, without their help and guidance along the way, this project would have been impossible. Dr. Jonathan House provided me plenty of rope to get myself in trouble however his ability to ask the right questions at the right time ensured I stayed on track throughout the process. His lifelong dedication to research and teaching enabled me the freedom to work the project knowing he was a simple call away. Dr. House, I am indebted to you. Mr. Stephen Brown and Ms. Elizabeth Bochtler provided expert assistance throughout the process and allowed me the freedom to create this thesis free of arbitrary deadlines. Ms. Bochtler, without your initial guidance I know I would still be juggling for a focused topic. Thank you for your insight and willingness to see me through the process. Mr. Brown, much like your instruction throughout the year, you allowed me to run with my ideas and were always there to provide a course correction when needed, thanks for stepping up and taking part in this project.

Next, I would like to thank Dr. Rhoda Risner and Ms. Venita Krueger. I was fortunate enough to be placed in Dr. Risner's A211 and A221 classes and could not have asked for a better professor. Dr. Risner, the way you provided information in a very professional manner was greatly appreciated by your students. Thank you for the subtle messages throughout the year reminding me to keep conducting research. Every time I saw a message from you it rekindled the fire and reminded me to stop being lazy. Ms. Krueger, year after year you get to take on the project of helping hundreds of people complete their thesis and without you, no one would accomplish this feat. Thanks for making the process as easy as possible. Your dedication to the professional appearance of this thesis is greatly appreciated.

I would like to give special thanks to my family. My Dad was a thesis away from completing his Master's degree many years ago. He provided the motivation needed to complete this project. To my wife Jessica thanks for your enduring support. Coming off a yearlong deployment to attend this course and work on this degree meant that my time with you was limited at best. Thanks for always being so supportive and allowing me to chase these crazy dreams. To my daughter Malia and son Michael Jr., thanks for making noise and creating the many disruptions while I was typing this thesis. You living life added another challenge to the project, one I accepted with a smile on my face.

Most importantly, my thanks and praise is always to God, for without Him nothing is possible.

TABLE OF CONTENTS

ACRONYMS

AFISRA	Air Force Intelligence, Surveillance and Reconnaissance Agency
CGI	Coast Guard Intelligence
CIA	Central Intelligence Agency
DCI	Director of Central Intelligence
DHS	Department of Homeland Security
DIA	Defense Intelligence Agency
DNI	Director of National Intelligence
DOD	Department of Defense
DOS	Department of State
FBI	Federal Bureau of Investigation
I&A	Intelligence and Analysis
IC	Intelligence Community
INSCOM	Army Intelligence and Security Command
IRTPA	Intelligence Reform and Terrorism Prevention Act
MCIA	Marine Corps Intelligence Activity
NGA	National Geospatial-Intelligence Agency
NRO	National Reconnaissance Office
NSA	National Security Agency
ODNI	Office of the Director of National Intelligence
OICI	Office of Intelligence and Counterintelligence
ONI	Office of Naval Intelligence
TFI	Terrorism and Financial Intelligence
USD (I)	Undersecretary of Defense for Intelligence

ILLUSTRATIONS

CHAPTER 1

INTRODUCTION AND OVERVIEW

Background

It is early fall of 2001, a very peaceful time of year; the holiday season was just around the corner. Seasons began to change, and the pace of life was slowing just a little. The author was a college senior finishing an undergraduate degree and looking forward to joining the United States Army in a short eight months. Early one morning the author arrived at a criminal justice class, unaware of the events that would change the lives of everyone in the world. 0846, impact—The North Tower of the World Trade Center was struck by an airplane. 0903, impact—The South Tower of the World Trade Center was struck by an airplane. 0937, impact—An airplane carrying 59 people crashed into the Western side of the Pentagon. 1003, impact—Forty four passengers on another aircraft crashed in Shanksville, Pennsylvania. How do these memories sit in your mind? This day, 11 September 2001, changed the lives of all Americans as well as the rest of the world. Two thousand, nine hundred and seventy seven innocent people lost their lives that day due to a cowardly act,[1] an act that would define the focus of the United States of America for the next 13 years. Security across the country tightened as the American people, despite differences in religious preference, race, political party affiliation, or social status, banded together as one team to care for each other. Phones were ringing off the hook and the Intelligence Community (IC) was faced with answering numerous

---

[1]History.com, "9/11 Attacks," http://www.history.com/topics/9-11-attacks (accessed 8 November 2013).

questions. Why did this happen? Why did the most powerful nation on earth not see this coming?

As the members of the IC began to scramble to answers questions, many people started to speculate concerning what happened. How could terrorists strike in our own backyard? Why did we not have answers prior to the attacks? In the aftermath of these tragic events, the members of the IC banded together to answer these questions. As it turns out, there were answers to many of the questions that were not distributed across the community. The community was holding information from each other in the name of secrecy. The IC had at least partial answers but kept those answers from the people that needed them the most. What was identified was a need for a reform, a need to change how the community operates.[2]

Gathering and sharing intelligence is crucial to military mission accomplishment, to preventing global war, and more importantly to ensuring our national security. While intelligence is commonly compartmentalized, there are occasions where the benefits of sharing compartmentalized intelligence far outweigh the risks. The IC commonly takes the blame when there is a failure to foresee actions against our interests at home and abroad. Members of the IC habitually keep information from each other in the name of secrecy and because of differing missions. For example, the FBI seeks to build a legal case against individual perpetrators, a task that requires a very high standard of proof while restricting access to its information so as to prevent suspects from learning of the investigation. The FBI is therefore, understandably, reluctant to increase the number of

---

[2]Public Law 108-458, *Intelligence Reform and Terrorism Prevention Act of 2004,* 17 December 2004, https://it.ojp.gov/default.aspx?area=privacy&page=1282# contentTop (accessed 4 November 2013).

people with access to this information. While it appears that intelligence sharing amongst members of the community has increased since the Intelligence Reform and Terrorism Prevention Act of 2004 (IRTPA), the author strongly believes the overall effectiveness of that sharing has room for improvement. The author believes the IRTPA of 2004 had valid recommendations that have not been implemented or have been overlooked throughout the community.

This thesis seeks to identify the ways in which the sharing of information between the members of the Intelligence Community has improved since the Intelligence Reform and Terrorism Prevention Act of 2004. It will also answer some background questions to demonstrate what problems have been addressed as well as try and identify recommendations on further improvement. This thesis will describe the composition of the IC and how the various agencies were aligned prior to the reform as well as how they are aligned today. The author will review recommendations that were made prior to the reform and try to identify why those recommendations were not implemented. This thesis will summarize the details of the reform, specifically Title I, and cover the details of what issues the reform identified. The author will cover the major changes that were proposed prior to 2004 and then highlight those changes that were made as a result of the reform. This thesis will attempt to explain why some recommendations were not implemented. Lastly, the author will describe how the IC worked prior to the reform and how the reform has changed the way intelligence is shared today. To conclude, the author will present recommendations for improving the IC and recommendations for further research on the topic.

This topic was chosen because there are problems in the IC that have been identified and recommendations made that have yet to be implemented. Some of these recommendations date back to over forty years ago.[3] As an intelligence officer who has been engaged in combat operations for the duration of his entire military career with an undergraduate degree in Criminal Justice, the author feels strongly that his educational background coupled with his military background clearly demonstrates firsthand knowledge of the questions proposed above and some potential solutions to the problems. While the Intelligence Reform and Terrorism Prevention Act of 2004 was instituted nine years ago, this topic is as relevant now as it was back when it was first looked at in 2001 and implemented in 2004. The consumers of intelligence deserve accurate and timely intelligence from the IC, both to protect U.S. national security as well as to protect the military forces throughout the world.

The Research Question

The primary research question to be answered in this thesis is: In what ways has the sharing of information between the members of the Intelligence Community improved since the Intelligence Reform and Terrorism Prevention Act of 2004?

In order to address this question, there are multiple questions that must be answered first in order to fully understand the background of this problem. The first theme, "Intelligence Community Construct," corresponds to secondary research questions one, How is the IC aligned today, and two, How was the IC aligned prior to IRTPA of

---

[3]Larry C. Kindsvater, "The Need to Reorganize the Intelligence Community A Senior Officer's Perspective," *Studies in Intelligence* 47, no. 1 (2003), http://www.cia.gov (accessed 3 November 2013).

2004, and will address the IC alignment prior to IRTPA and currently in 2014. The second theme, "Intelligence Community Issues Identified", corresponds to research questions three, What issues were identified prior to the IRTPA of 2004?, and four, What issues were identified by IRTPA of 2004? The second theme will focus on issues within the IC prior to IRTPA and issues that were identified as a result of the reform act. The third theme, "Change", relates to secondary research questions five, what changes were made based on IRTPA of 2004, and six, what changes were not made, and this theme will answer those questions while trying to address why changes that were recommended were not implemented. The final theme, "Intelligence Sharing," addresses the final two secondary questions, seven, How was intelligence shared amongst the IC prior to IRTPA?, and eight, How is intelligence shared today?

Assumptions

This thesis assumes that there are no imminent major changes to the national level or defense level intelligence structure. The author assumes there are no current recommendations that reside in either chamber of the United States Congress awaiting a vote. This thesis also assumes that the Intelligence Reform and Terrorism Prevention Act of 2004 has in fact made some positive changes to the way the community operates. Most importantly, the author assumes that changes to the IC that will benefit all members are welcomed amongst the community and that those members are willing to put the cultural differences aside to benefit the entire community.

Definitions

Some of the terms used throughout this thesis will be defined in this paragraph.

Intelligence Community (IC)—The Intelligence Community is comprised of 17 members. The Central Intelligence Agency (CIA) is an independent agency. The Department of Defense includes the Defense Intelligence Agency (DIA), National Security Agency (NSA), National Geospatial-Intelligence Agency (NGA), National Reconnaissance Office (NRO), Army Intelligence and Security Command (INSCOM), Air Force Intelligence, Surveillance and Reconnaissance Agency (AFISRA), Marine Corps Intelligence Activity (MCIA), and Office of Naval Intelligence (ONI). The United States Department of Energy has the Office of Intelligence and Counterintelligence (OICI). The United States Department of Homeland Security is comprised of the Office of Intelligence and Analysis (I&A) and Coast Guard Intelligence (CGI).

The United States Department of Justice consists of the Federal Bureau of Investigation, National Security Branch (FBI/NSB), and the Drug Enforcement Administration, Office of National Security Intelligence (DEA/ONSI). The United States Department of State has the Bureau of Intelligence and Research (INR), while the United States Department of the Treasury has the Office of Terrorism and Financial Intelligence (TFI). The head of the Intelligence Community is the Director of National Intelligence (DNI) who also directs the Office of the Director of National Intelligence (ODNI). Members of the IC collect and assess information regarding international terrorist and narcotic activities; other hostile activities by foreign powers, organizations, persons, and their agents; and foreign intelligence activities directed against the United States (U.S.).

As needed, the President of the United States may also direct the IC to carry out special activities in order to protect U.S. security interests against foreign threats.[4]

Limitations and Delimitations

In order to ensure this thesis might be distributed across the community, the author kept its contents unclassified. By keeping this unclassified, the author realizes the limitations on material regarding the changes being made inside the IC. As a result of this thesis remaining at the unclassified level, the author knowingly did not conduct any research in the classified realm in order to ensure that no spillage occurred. While the author will give a brief background of the problem to be addressed, this thesis will focus on changes that have been made to the IC post the IRTPA of 2004 and its implementation. By limiting the focus to the sharing of information amongst the members of the IC post the IRTPA of 2004, the author knowingly does not cover other issues that remain in the IC and can be researched in further studies.

Significance of the Study

The effective sharing of intelligence across the members of the IC has been a topic of discussion for many years. This thesis seeks to identify the recommended changes as a result of the IRTPA of 2004, identify the changes that were made, study the effectiveness of those changes, and identify what changes have yet to be made. In conducting the research, the author intends to make potential recommendations that could have a lasting impact on the IC. The recommendations are meant to address a problem

---

[4]Intelligence.gov, "Mission of the Intelligence Community," http://Intelligence. gov/mission (accessed 4 November 2013).

and are not specifically directed at those persons responsible for drafting the current laws that govern the IC.

The next chapter will review a variety of literature that was used to answer the proposed questions. The next chapter will continue the structure that was introduced in this chapter to better organize all significant materials used.

CHAPTER 2

LITERATURE REVIEW

Strategic intelligence allows anticipation or prediction of future situations and circumstances, and it informs the decisions of senior members of the United States Government.[5] It is this intelligence that ensures the people of the United States and their allies remain safe. Accurate intelligence collection is the goal of all members of the IC. Intelligence drives operations in the United States military and it helps policy makers and ultimately the President of the United States make informed decisions regarding the national security of the United States of America both in the homeland and abroad.

The purpose of this thesis is to identify the ways that intelligence sharing has improved between members of the IC since the signing of the IRTPA of 2004.

This chapter, the literature review, provides the framework to answer the primary and secondary research questions. As introduced in the previous chapter, the themes used in this chapter will be consistent. This will assist the reader and future researchers when seeking answers to specific questions. The author used many sources that contributed to the conclusions and recommendations made in the final chapter. It is the main sources that will be discussed in detail in this chapter. Some of the literature helped to answer more than one secondary question. Those sources will be listed in the first category that they apply to and will be excluded from the others.

The author used many different types of literature in order to fully understand the magnitude of this project and enabled the recommendations made in chapter 5. In order

---

[5]Joint Chiefs of Staff, Joint Publication 2-0, *Joint Intelligence* (Washington, DC: Government Printing Office, 2007).

9

to ensure effective research was accomplished, the author used testimony from senior members of the IC, testimony from members of the United States Congress, U.S. Public Law and Presidential Executive Orders, as well as many books, journals, and online articles. From U.S. Public Law and Executive Orders to online articles, the author attempted to gather and corroborate information across a wide spectrum of sources.

Using the themes already introduced, the author will cover important literature from this research project.

Intelligence Community Construct

In his article on "Overhauling Intelligence," the author, Admiral Mike McConnell, points out that the *National Security Act of 1947* mandated that intelligence be shared up the chain of command but not horizontally. This statement clearly defines the problems that exist in the IC. At the time that he wrote "Overhauling Intelligence," McConnell was the Director of National Intelligence (DNI). As the most senior member in the IC, with the mission of improving intelligence integrations across the IC, his view clearly demonstrates a need for improvement. McConnell notes that the IRTPA of 2004, namely the creation of the DNI, was crucial to reforming the IC, however, without some additional changes the act itself is inefficient. He thinks the IC should increase their agility and begin to coordinate amongst other members more effectively. He discusses the purpose of creating the DNI position, to focus, guide, and coordinate the other sixteen members of the IC to provide timely and accurate, tailored intelligence to policy makers.

McConnell references the *National Security Act of 1947* and its goal of bringing U.S. military and foreign intelligence together but he sees a fault where that law failed to account for the integration of intelligence and law enforcement. This failure was addressed in the IRTPA of 2004 with the creation of six intelligence centers. McConnell

discusses some recommendations on how to improve the IC, starting with an overall

culture change. He describes how the members of the IC have very unique missions that

are all governed by separate rules and regulations. This separation of missions and

different rules helps keep the divide between the members of the IC. McConnell

recommends that, much like the U.S. military has moved to joint formations, the IC

should also use this model to begin to open the doors within the community to more

resemble military formations. This article cites the coordination between the FBI's

National Security Branch and the Department of Homeland Security (DHS) as a success

story, addressing at least one of the issues in the *National Security Act of 1947*. These two

members of the IC effectively work together daily to protect the United States from

domestic and/or international terrorist attacks.[6]

Intelligence Community Issues Identified

In order to identify the issues that were present within the IC, the author

researched four Executive Orders. These orders enabled the author to see what issues

were identified and evaluate the proposed changes made. The primary Executive Orders

that were significant in the research of the project include Executive Order 11905, *United

States Foreign Intelligence Activities*, Executive Order 12333, *United States Intelligence

Activities*, and Executive Order 13555, *Strengthened Management of the Intelligence

Community.*

---

[6]Mike McConnell, "Overhauling Intelligence," *Foreign Affairs* 86, no. 4
(July/August 2007).

The IRTPA of 2004, most notably, created the position of the DNI as the head of the IC. This is a drastic change from Executive Order 11905, *United States Foreign Intelligence Activities*, which President Gerald Ford signed in 1976 naming the Director of Central Intelligence (DCI) as the senior intelligence advisor to the President of the United States.[7] These responsibilities now fall on the DNI.

Executive Order 12333, *United States Intelligence Activities*, is the principal guiding order for the IC. President Ronald Reagan, in 1981, issued this order that detailed the duties and responsibilities of the IC. President Reagan was responsible for increasing the powers and responsibilities of the members of the IC as well as directing all federal agencies to cooperate with the requests for information originating in the CIA. Executive Order 12333, though it has been amended, is still in effect today.[8]

Executive Order 13355, *Strengthened Management of the Intelligence Community*, was signed by President George W. Bush in August of 2004. This Executive Order therefore took effect four months prior to the IRTPA of 2004. This Executive Order strengthened the authority of the DCI while charging the position with the responsibility of integrating intelligence collection activities across the IC. The DCI was also named the principal advisor to the President of the United States as well as the National Security Council and the Homeland Security Council. These duties and

---

[7] White House, Executive Order 11905, *United States Foreign Intelligence Activities,* Federal Register, 18 February 1976, http://www.archives.gov/federal-register/executive-orders/ (accessed 18 March 2014).

[8] White House, Executive Order 12333, *United States Intelligence Activities.* Federal Register, 4 December 1981, http://www.archives.gov/federal-register/executive-orders/ (accessed 18 March 2014).

responsibilities would be transferred to the newly created DNI with the signing of the IRTPA of 2004 in December of the same year.[9]

The *9/11 Commission Report: Final Report of the National Commission on Terrorist Attacks upon the United States* covers all agencies in the IC and their functions. This commission identified the need for a single position in charge of all intelligence activities.[10] While this recommendation has been made on many occasions, it is the author's belief that the change was finally made as a result of the attacks on the United States in September 2001.

Change

The author used many sources of information in seeking to answer the primary research question and make recommended changes to benefit the IC. Of note, the Intelligence Reform and Terrorism Prevention Act of 2004 was used as the baseline to analyze the directed changes to the IC. This study addresses many different aspects of the IC, most notably reorganization and the creation of the DNI position. Creating the DNI position also formed the Office of the Director of National Intelligence (ODNI), a seventeenth member to the IC.[11]

---

[9]White House, Executive Order 13355, *Strengthened Management of the Intelligence Community,* Federal Register, 27 August 2004, http://www.archives.gov/federal-register/executive-orders/ (accessed 18 March 2014).

[10]National Commission on Terrorist Attacks Upon the United States, *The 9/11 Commission Report: Final Report of the National Commission on Terrorist Attacks Upon the United States* (Washington, DC: GPO, 2004), 357.

[11]Public Law 108-458, *Intelligence Reform and Terrorism Prevention Act of 2004*, 17 December 2004.

Intelligence Reform, 2001-2009: Requiescat in Pace? is an article by Patrick C. Neary that suggests history is repeating itself with the IRTPA of 2004. Neary mentions the comparison between the events that occurred on 7 December 1941 and the subsequent *National Security Act of 1947* that created the CIA and the events on 11 September 2001 and the drafting of the IRTPA of 2004. Neary suggests that the IRTPA was a compromise that took place on the floors of Congress. Neary references that Senators Susan Collins (R-ME) and Joe Lieberman (D-CT) came to a bipartisan agreement that the IC needed one person in charge of all intelligence activities. In the House of Representatives, this was seen as taking powers away from the DOD and thus the compromise was a new figurehead, the DNI, who did not have the authority to affect any existing members of the IC.

Neary suggests there are three conditions that will work to stop the reorganization of the IC: conflicting motivations in those considering it, environmental challenges at initiation, and failures in leadership. While he can see reform working, Neary suggests that some difficult choices need to be made when the opportunity arises. The 9/11 commission suggested changing the IC and making it more centralized. Even though IRTPA formed the DNI position, it also included language that would limit the power of the DNI. Creating a position and not giving the proper authorities is hardly reform. Neary says the single biggest impediment of reform was the lack of a clear mission for the ODNI.[12]

---

[12]Patrick C. Neary, "'Intelligence Reform', 2001-2009: Requiescat in Pace?" *Studies in Intelligence* 54, no. 1 (March 2010).

The Office of the Director of National Intelligence's Office of the Inspector General produced *Critical Intelligence Community Management Challenges,* a report published on 12 November 2008 that clearly outlined the roles and functions of the DNI. This report shows that the IRTPA of 2004 charged the DNI with not only leading the IC but transforming it while serving as the principal intelligence advisor to the President of the United States and the National Security Council. This report highlighted the DNI's overall responsibility for the sharing of intelligence. In its findings, the report stated that sharing of intelligence problems will continue until the IC creates policies and process on information sharing and implements those policies. This report recommended the DNI take three steps to advance collaboration and integration in the IC: have all members of the IC work together on programs, systems, and acquisitions, order the IC to comply with the decisions of the DNI, and appoint a senior ODNI official responsible for improving collaboration between traditional members of the IC and those that have law enforcement responsibilities, FBI and DHS.[13]

Intelligence Sharing

"The Need to Reorganize the Intelligence Community, A Senior Officer's Perspective" by Larry C. Kindsvater discussed recommended changes from a then senior member of the IC. Larry Kindsvater was the Executive Director of Intelligence Community Affairs. His article discussed fundamental changes that were needed to improve the way the IC functioned. He noted that during the past fifty years there have

---

[13]Edward Maguire, *Critical Intelligence Community Managing Challenges* (Washington, DC: Office of the Director of National Intelligence, 12 November 2008), http://www.fas.org/irp/news/2009/04/odni-ig-1108.pdf (accessed 22 January 2014).

been over twenty official commissions and executive branch studies that made proposals to improve the IC. This clearly demonstrates the depth of this problem. He stated that because of these issues, the IC is not managed or organized to address national security missions and threats. The goal of true intelligence reform is to end the stove pipes that plague the community, however Kindsvater notes that collection is still "stove piped" and dissemination is even more compartmentalized. The stove pipes are at the national level and Kindsvater suggest these stoves pipes were created based on the type of intelligence gathered, for example NSA dealing with signals intelligence (SIGINT) and the CIA and DIA dealing with human intelligence (HUMINT).[14] Until these arbitrary walls are broken down, true intelligence reform won't be successful.

Other Information

In conducting research on this topic, the author reviewed two published Masters of Military Arts and Science theses that were written at the U.S. Army Command and General Staff College. This information gives a different perspective on topics that are closely related to the primary research question.

In 2006, Heinisha S. Jacques researched the effectiveness of the ODNI. She concluded that the DNI can be effective if given the proper resources to execute the job.
[15]

---

[14]Kindsvater, "The Need to Reorganize the Intelligence Community A Senior Officer's Perspective."

[15]Heinisha S. Jacques, "Director of National Intelligence: Another Bureaucratic Layer or an Effective Officer?" (Master's Thesis, U.S. Army Command and General Staff College, 2006).

In 2011, Army Major William T. Wilburn researched the role of the Undersecretary of Defense for Intelligence (USD (I)) and how that position should complement the IC reform. He concluded that the USD (I) is not properly postured to complement the authorities of the DNI thus resulting in marginal improvements to the IC.[16]

Both of these prior research projects reached similar conclusions; intelligence reform is not complete nor will it be until the DNI is given proper authorities to lead the IC.

---

[16]William T. Wilburn, "The Under Secretary of Defense for Intelligence: Posturing Authorities to Complement Intelligence Community Reform" (Master's Thesis, U.S. Army Command and General Staff College, 2011).

CHAPTER 3

RESEARCH METHODOLOGY

The main purpose of this study is to identify the ways that the sharing of information between the members of the Intelligence Community has improved since the Intelligence Reform and Terrorism Prevention Act of 2004. The research will address recommendations that were made prior to the IRTPA as well as cover the changes that were made as a result of that law. By studying the changes made, the author intends to gauge the effectiveness of those changes by comparing the IC prior to the change to the IC as it is currently structured.

This chapter will cover the methods used to conduct the research and enabled the author to gain information that helped answer the primary and secondary research questions. The author intends to do a qualitative analysis using material published about the IC. The author will also use the IRTPA of 2004 as well as numerous pages of testimony from senior members of the IC.

The following discussion covers the organizational structure of the IC both pre- and post-2004 reconfiguration. The organizational structure will allow the reader to visualize the composition of the IC prior to the IRTPA of 2004 and generally understand how information was shared. Once the reader understands how the IC operated in the past it allows comparisons to be made with how the IC operates today. Comparing the flow of information from pre—and post—2004 and analyzing the IC structures will identify gaps in information flow and begin to answer the primary research question. Using this research, this study makes recommendations on how to improve the sharing of information while pointing out the improvements from the initiation of the IRTPA of 2004 to present day.

In order to begin to answer the primary research question, the study includes testimony from senior members of the IC, both past and present. By using these articles and testimony, the author was able to gather insight from those who were in positions to help influence change within the community. This research, by pointing out the improvements, also identified the shortcomings based on the changes made. Those shortcomings provided the basis for the recommendations in chapter 5 of this thesis.

The author used his personal experience working in the IC to compare how intelligence was shared prior to the IRTPA of 2004 to how it is working today. Using qualitative methods of research, the author compared articles and recommendations from as far back as 1949 up to articles and testimony given in the past three years, keeping the focus on information since the IRTPA of 2004.

Instead of gathering information in the form of a survey, the author relied on articles written by former leaders in the IC. As a result of this method not being used, the author made the recommendation for further research in the final chapter of this thesis.

This research method has some inherent weaknesses. First, the author has limited access to the most senior members of the IC that may have useful information to help answer the primary research question. Because of this limited access, the author was unable to conduct face to face interviews to gather further information as to why some decisions were made and others were ignored. Due to this thesis remaining at the unclassified level, the author did not attempt to gather any information from classified sources in order to prevent spillage. All information in this thesis is unclassified and should classified information exist, this thesis will not address that information.

The next chapter will cover each secondary research question. The author will provide an explanation of the answers for each question and detail how the secondary questions further enabled the answering of the primary research question. The analysis conducted in the next chapter enabled the author to answer the primary question, detail the improvements to the sharing of information in the IC since the IRTPA of 2004, and make recommendations to continue to improve the IC and improve information sharing amongst the community. This analysis also enabled the author to make recommendations for further research on the topic.

CHAPTER 4

ANALYSIS

For many years, the IC has been blamed for failing to identify potential threats to the United States. These accusations generally come to light after a significant act of terrorism or another major event occurs and the blame is placed on a lack of accurate intelligence. Usually, when these events happen, the IC is blamed for not sharing information amongst its members that could have prevented the situation from happening. A majority of the public fails to realize that intelligence has numerous attacks because of the work of the men and women in the IC. Success in the IC goes unrecognized while failure becomes public knowledge. Since the IRTPA of 2004, the IC has been directed to increase sharing amongst the community.[17] Increased sharing is something the author believes if happening today.

The purpose of this study is to identify the ways that intelligence sharing has improved between members of the IC since the signing of the IRTPA of 2004.

The purpose of this chapter is to analyze the data gathered using the themes introduced during the literature review in chapter two. The first theme, Intelligence Community Construct, corresponds to secondary research questions one, How is the IC aligned today, and two, how was the IC aligned prior to IRTPA of 2004, and will address the IC alignment prior to IRTPA and currently in 2014. The second theme, Intelligence Community Issues, corresponds to research questions three, What issues were identified prior to the IRTPA of 2004, and four, What issues were identified by the IRTPA of 2004

---

[17]Public Law 108-458, *Intelligence Reform and Terrorism Prevention Act of 2004*, 17 December 2004.

21

and will focus on issues within the IC prior to IRTPA and issues that were identified as a result of the reform act. The third theme, Change, relates to secondary research questions five, what changes were made based on the IRTPA of 2004, and six, what changes were not made, and this theme will answer those questions while trying to address why changes that were recommended were not implemented. The final theme, Intelligence Sharing, addresses the final two secondary questions, seven, How was intelligence shared amongst the IC prior to the IRTPA, and eight, How is intelligence shared today? In looking at these questions, the researcher was able to understand the differences between what was and what is and formulate an opinion as to why the IC operates the way it does today.

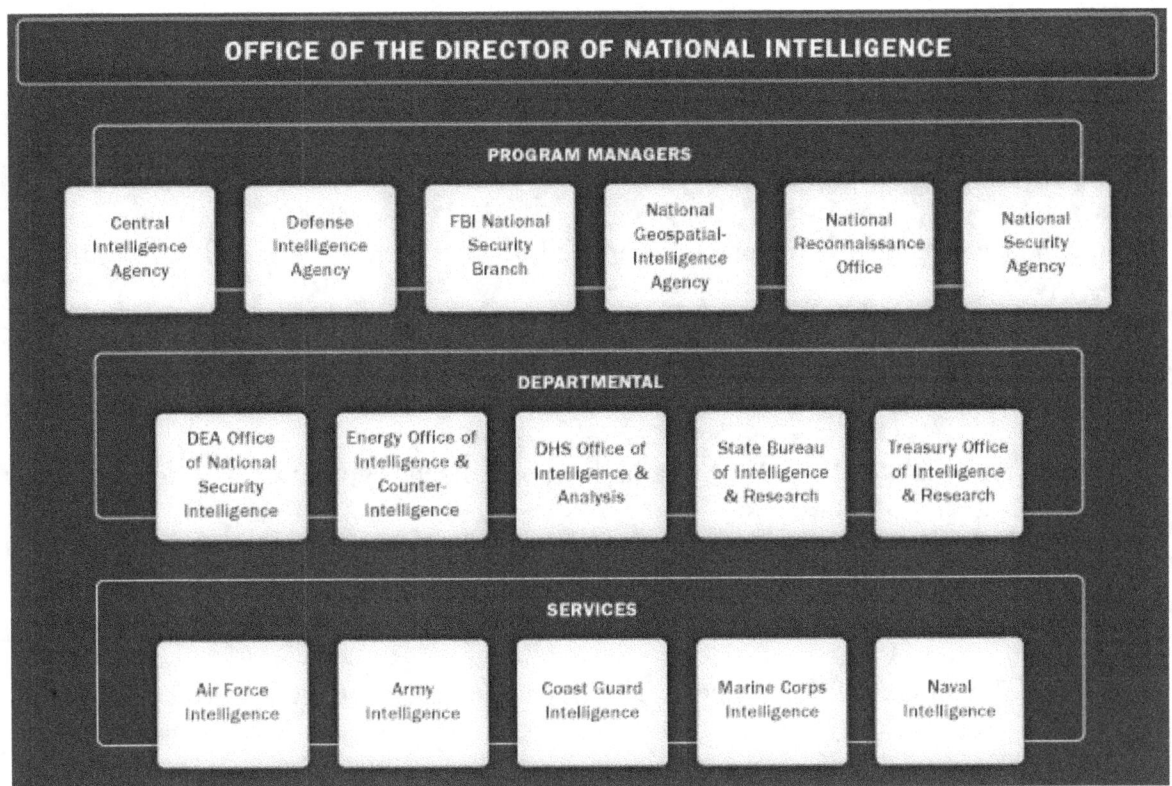

Figure 1.   Intelligence Community Organizational Chart

Source: Intelligence.gov, "A Complex Organization United under a Single Goal: National Security," http://www.intelligence.gov/mission/structure.html (accessed 16 March 2014).

Intelligence Community Construct

How is the Intelligence Community Aligned Today?

Today, the IC consists of seventeen organizations, all under the direction of the ODNI. The DNI was given the mission to lead intelligence integration across the community. This mission came as a direct result of the IRTPA of 2004. The researcher considers the ODNI as a member of the IC. A brief description of the other members of the IC will follow.

The CIA is an independent agency responsible for providing national security intelligence to senior U.S. policymakers. The CIA is led by the DCI who formally held the responsibility of leading the IC.

The Department of Defense is comprised of eight members of the IC. The DIA is a combat support agency responsible for producing and managing foreign military intelligence and providing that intelligence to the warfighter on the ground as well as to the defense policymakers. The NSA is a highly specialized cryptologic organization that is responsible for coordinating, directing, and performing activities aimed at protecting U.S. information systems as well as identifying threat signals. The NGA is responsible for geospatial intelligence that supports overall national security. NGA performs their mission by creating tailored solutions to both military and civilian leadership. The NRO is responsible for designing and building the nation's satellites and providing the information produced by those satellites to both military and civilian leadership. This information serves to provide early warning of potential trouble, assists military commanders in planning operations, and monitors the environment. INSCOM is responsible for all intelligence activities within the Department of the Army to include oversight. The AFISRA provides policy, guidance, and oversight to all intelligence organizations in the Air Force. The MCIA is responsible for providing operational and tactical level intelligence support to all Marine Corps intelligence professionals. This support includes guidance, policy and budgeting. The ONI provides maritime intelligence to all components of the U.S Navy and joint warfighters. ONI also provides intelligence support to national level policy makers and other members of the IC.

The United States Department of Energy has the OICI. The OICI is responsible for providing intelligence and counterintelligence for all of the Department of Energy to include thirty offices nationwide. The main responsibility is to protect scientific data including national security information and technologies.

The United States Department of Homeland Security includes the Office of I&A and Coast Guard Intelligence (CGI). I&A uses information and intelligence from other members of the IC to assess current and future threats to the U.S. homeland. CGI is responsible for protecting the citizens of the United States by ensuring their maritime safety, maritime security, and protecting the ocean through maritime stewardship. Because of their unique authorities and mission, CGI provides intelligence to the Coast Guard as well as national level leaders.

The United States Department of Justice consists of the Federal Bureau of Investigation, National Security Branch (FBI/NSB), and the Drug Enforcement Administration, Office of National Security Intelligence (DEA/ONSI). The FBI/NSB is a unique intelligence and law enforcement agency responsible for understanding threats to U.S. national security while working to provide that information to national level authorities as well as state and local law enforcement. DEA/ONSI is responsible for enforcing laws and regulations regarding to controlled substances. This organization shares intelligence amongst the IC to reduce the amount of drugs in the United States as well as to combat global terrorism.

The United States Department of State has the Bureau of Intelligence and Research (INR). INR provides the Secretary of State with current analysis of global situations allowing for immediate response should the need arise.

The United States Department of the Treasury has the Office of Terrorism and Financial Intelligence (TFI). TFI is also responsible for foreign intelligence and counterintelligence related to operations and responsibilities of the Department of Transportation. The main mission is to safeguard the financial system from all national security threats.[18]

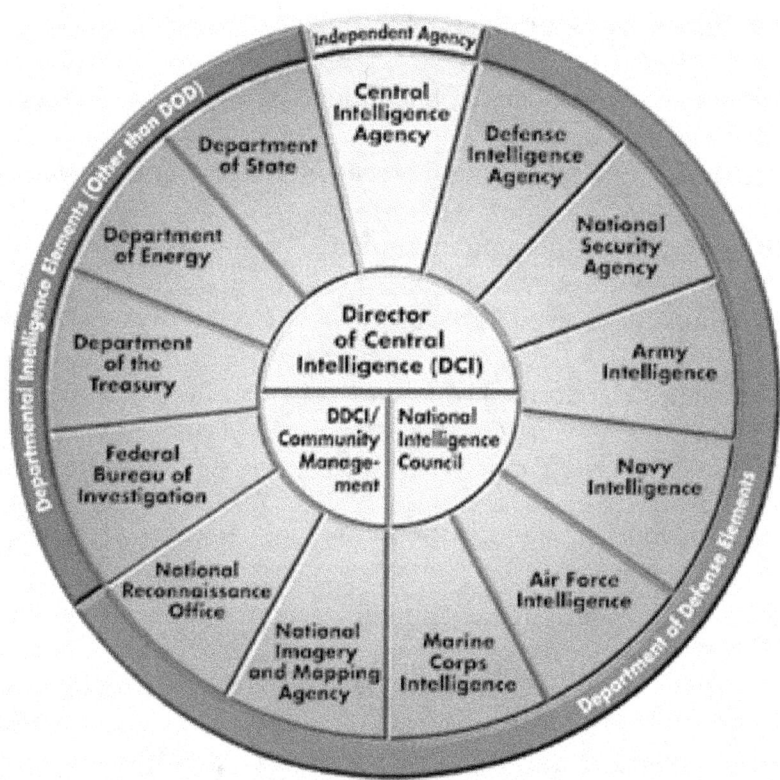

Figure 2.   Intelligence Community prior to the Intelligence Reform and Terrorism Prevention Act of 2004

Source: Central Intelligence Agency, "Intelligence Community," www.fas.org/irp/cia/product/facttell/intcomm.htm (accessed 16 March 2014).

---

[18]Office of the Director of National Intelligence, "Members of the Intelligence Community," http://www.dni.gov/index.php/intelligence-community/members-of-the-ic (accessed 19 March 2014).

How was the Intelligence Community aligned prior to the
Intelligence Reform and Terrorism Prevention Act of 2004?

Prior to the IRTPA of 2004, the IC consisted of thirteen members under the

supervision of the Director of Central Intelligence (DCI). While the DCI still maintained

duties as the leader of the CIA, he also performed functions as the senior intelligence

advisor to the President of the United States. This structure has been in place since the

National Security Act of 1947 when the CIA was formed. Today, the IC has seventeen

members; the four members that were not part of the IC prior to the reform are ODNI,

DHS, DEA, and the CGI.[19]

Intelligence Community Issues Identified

What Issues were identified prior to the Intelligence Reform
and Terrorism Prevention Act of 2004?

There were many recommended changes to the IC prior to the IRTPA of 2004.

Despite the intent of these suggestions to improve the IC, none of these changes were

made. Below are six examples of recommended changes that may have improved the

overall effectiveness of the IC prior to the major reform in 2004 and potentially could

have prevented the terrorist attacks in 2001 and in previous years.

In 1949, 55 years prior to the IRTPA of 2004, the first Hoover Commission

demanded that the CIA be the one central agency responsible for the entire national

intelligence community.

---

[19]McConnell, "Overhauling Intelligence,"49-58.

In 1955 the second Hoover Commission made a recommendation, similar to the duties of the current DNI that would place the DCI in charge of the IC and have his second in charge, deputy, oversee the functions of the CIA.

In 1971 the Schlesinger Report first recommended a DNI by title however the report did not go as far in saying that the DNI should be responsible for the CIA. Thus, his authority would not exceed the DCI thereby making two senior members with roughly the same duties.

In 1976 the Church Committee recommended all funding for the IC be put under the responsibility of the DCI. This committee also recommended removing the DCI from the CIA and placing this position in charge of the IC.[20]

Again in 1976 a former Secretary of Defense, Clark Clifford, who was responsible for the initial draft legislation that created the CIA, made a recommendation similar to forming the DNI, calling it the Director of General Intelligence. He suggested that this additional position be created and be separate from the DCI.[21]

In 1992 Senator David Boren and Representative David McCurdy suggested a DNI with full authority over the IC to include the ability to transfer people amongst the agencies within the community. While there were varying details in each of their plans, both agreed that there was a need for an additional position to oversee the IC.[22]

---

[20]U.S. Senate, "U.S. Senate Select Committee on Intelligence," http://www.intelligence.senate.gov/churchcommittee.html (accessed 20 March 2014).

[21]The Robinson Library, "Clark Clifford," http://www.robinsonlibrary.com/america/unitedstates/1961/biography/clifford-c.htm (accessed 21 March 2014).

[22]James Burch, "The Domestic Intelligence Gap: Progress Since 9/11?" *Homeland Security Affair*, 2008, http://www.hsaj.org/?special:fullarticle=supplement.2.2 (accessed 20 March 2014).

Executive Orders

President Gerald Ford, in 1976, issued Executive Order 11905 that named the DCI as the senior intelligence advisor to the President of the United States.[23]

In 1978, President Jimmy Carter issued Executive Order 12036 that further defined the responsibilities of the DCI.[24] President Ronald Reagan, in 1981, issued Executive Order 12333 that again further detailed the duties and responsibilities of the IC. President Reagan was responsible for increasing the powers and responsibilities of the members of the IC as well as directing all federal agencies to cooperate with the requests for information originating in the CIA. Executive Order 12333, though it has been amended, is still in effect today.[25]

President George W. Bush signed Executive Order 13355, Strengthened Management of the Intelligence Community on August 27, 2004. This Executive Order is significant because it was signed four months prior to the IRTPA of 2004 and was issued to strengthen the authority of the DCI. It charged the DCI with integrating intelligence collection activities while naming him the principal advisor to the President of the United States as well as the National Security Council and Homeland Security Council. These duties would be transferred a short four months later to the new DNI.[26]

---

[23] White House, Executive Order 11905.

[24] White House, Executive Order 12036, *United States Intelligence Activities.* Federal Register, 24 January 1978, http://www.archives.gov/federal-register/executive-orders/ (accessed 18 March 2014).

[25] White House, Executive Order 12333.

[26] White House, Executive Order 13355.

Most of these issues were identified long before the IRTPA of 2004 and recommended changes were made throughout the years from the inception of the CIA with the *National Security Act of 1947* up to the reform in 2004. While the IRTPA of 2004 created the DNI, it did not go as far as some of the recommendations suggested in giving full authority over the IC to the DNI.[27]

What Issues were identified by the Intelligence Reform and Terrorism Prevention Act of 2004?

Public Law 108-458, dated 17 December 2004, is the *Intelligence Reform and Terrorism Prevention Act of 2004*. This law was signed by President George W. Bush and identified issues in many areas of the IC and made changes that will be discussed later in this chapter. The issues that were identified include:

Title I-Reform of the Intelligence Community

> Establishment of the Director of National Intelligence (DNI)

> Reorganization and improvement of the management of the IC

> Information Sharing

Title II-Federal Bureau of Investigation

> Improving intelligence capabilities of the FBI

Title III-Security Clearances

Title IV-Transportation Security

Title V-Border Protection, Immigration, and Visa matters

Title VI-Terrorism prevention

Title VII-Implementation of the 9/11 Commission Recommendations

---

[27]Kindsvater, "The Need to Reorganize the Intelligence Community," 2.

Diplomacy, Foreign aid, and the military war on terrorism

Homeland Security

Title VIII-Other matters.

The eight titles in the IRTPA of 2004 refocused the IC, gave new direction and authorities, and helped to restructure the IC. This thesis will focus on portions of Title I.[28]

<u>Change</u>

What Changes were made as a Result of the Intelligence Reform
and Terrorism Prevention Act of 2004?

Title I of the IRTPA of 2004 concerns the development of the DNI, the development of the ODNI, the establishment of the National Counterterrorism Center (NCTC), and the establishment of the National Counterproliferation Center (NCPC).[29]

The Director of National Intelligence is the senior intelligence advisor to the President of the United States, the National Security Council, and the Homeland Security Council, responsible for leading intelligence integration across the IC. After numerous attempts to form a position that places one person in charge of the entire IC, the IRTPA of 2004 finally addressed these concerns based on the recommendation of the 9/11 Commission Report. While the incumbent of this position is overall in charge of the IC and the IRTPA of 2004 stated that the DCI must report activities to the DNI, this continues to be a point of contention amongst the members of the IC.[30]

---

[28]Public Law 108-458, *Intelligence Reform and Terrorism Prevention Act of 2004*, 17 December 2004.

[29]Ibid., 7.

[30]Office of the Director of National Intelligence, "Mission," http://www.odni.gov/index.php/about/mission (accessed 21 March 2014).

The ODNI was formed to assist the DNI with his responsibilities. The ODNI is responsible for integrating foreign, military, and domestic intelligence in order to effectively defend the U.S homeland as well as U.S. interests abroad. Currently the ODNI is responsible for six centers focused on integrating intelligence across the IC: Intelligence Advanced Research Projects Agency (IARPA), Information Sharing Environment (ISE), National Counterterrorism Center (NCTC), National Counterproliferation Center (NCPC), National Intelligence Council (NIC), and the Office of the National Counterintelligence Executive (ONCIX).[31]

The National Counterterrorism Center (NCTC) was formerly the Terrorist Threat Integration Center (TTIC). The NCTC belongs to the ODNI and is responsible for analyzing terrorism intelligence, storing this intelligence, and planning counterterrorism activities in support of the DNI and U.S. national security interests.[32]

The National Counterproliferation Center (NCPC) was established as a result of the IRTPA of 2004 but was not officially formed until November 2005. This center is responsible for identifying gaps in knowledge as they pertain to weapons of mass destruction. These weapons can be chemical, nuclear, biological, or radiological in nature. This center also belongs to the ODNI and works closely with all members of the IC as well as other elements the U.S. government.[33]

---

[31]Office of the Director of National Intelligence, "Organization," http://www.odni.gov/index.php/about/organization (accessed 21 March 2014).

[32]National Counterterrorism Center, "Overview," http://www.nctc.gov/overview.html (accessed 17 March 2014).

[33]National Counterproliferation Center, Homepage, http://www.counterwmd.gov (accessed 17 March 2014).

What Changes were Recommended
but not made and why?

Despite the good inventions of the IRTPA of 2004, his research has identified one major change that was not implemented in the manner to which it was originally intended. In order to be truly effective, the DNI position needs to be given full authority over the IC. This authority should include management of all personnel, budgeting for the entire IC, and a direct reporting chain from all subordinate members to the ODNI. The DNI should be sufficiently empowered to transform the culture of the IC from a group of narrowly focused organizations to one that is willing to share information amongst the community for the benefit of the entire IC and not one specific member. As the current mandate stands today, the Department of Defense (DOD) is responsible for eight of the seventeen members of the IC. It is understandable that the military service members of the IC belong to the DOD, however, NSA, NGA, and NRO all fall under the DOD and do not report directly to the DNI. If the DNI is overall responsible for the IC then this position needs to have the latitude to place personnel, including military personnel assigned to any intelligence agency, in like positions across the community to better accomplish the mission of intelligence integration.[34]

Intelligence Sharing

How was Intelligence Shared Amongst the Intelligence Community prior to the Intelligence Reform and Terrorism Prevention Act of 2004?

Prior to the IRTPA of 2004, the IC was organized in a manner that had the DCI responsible for the entire community. While the DCI did not have the same

---

[34]Kindsvater, "The Need to Reorganize the Intelligence Community," 5.

responsibilities that the current DNI does, that director was at least nominally the leader of the community. The DCI was the senior intelligence advisor to the President of the United States and used his position to influence the community. Intelligence, while still compartmentalized, was more stove-piped. Due to the differences in culture and the differences in authorities and regulations guiding their function, each member of the IC conducted business in a different manner. While the community paid lip service to the sharing of intelligence, most information that was shared was done so within the specific entity. While liaison positions were present, these positions were not viewed as true intelligence integration but rather a way for one organization to obtain what it could from another agency to benefit the first organization's mission.[35]

How is Intelligence Shared Today?

Due to the changes in the organization of the IC, the sharing of intelligence today has changed drastically. Because of the IRTPA of 2004, six intelligence centers, under direct control of the DNI, were formed that forced each member of the IC to send representatives in order to participate in the mission. The DNI was assigned the mission of improving intelligence integration across community. The organization of the IC since the IRTPA of 2004 ensured that there is one person in charge of the community. As pointed out earlier in this research, the authorities of the DNI need to be modified to ensure that the DNI truly has control over the entire community.

---

[35]McConnell, "Overhauling Intelligence," 52-53.

CHAPTER 5

CONCLUSIONS AND RECOMMENDATIONS

Conclusions

This study's primary research question, in what ways have the sharing of information between the members of the Intelligence Community improved since the Intelligence Reform and Terrorism Prevention Act of 2004, was answered in several ways. It appears very clear that the sharing of information has improved since the IRTPA of 2004, but whether or not this improvement is directly attributed to the IRTPA of 2004 remains to be studied.

Director of National Intelligence

The first answer to the primary research question was the introduction of the Director of National Intelligence (DNI) to the intelligence community (IC) ensuring that one person is responsible for the functions of the IC. With the creation of the new position came two very pointed missions, improve the sharing of information amongst the community and serve as the senior intelligence advisor to the President of the United States. The mission of the DNI clearly states that the improvement of intelligence sharing is a top priority. While the IC now has one person in charge, there continues to be issues with the authorities granted to the DNI. This research has shown that the DNI, with the authorities as they currently stand, is more of a manager of the community as opposed to the director. Should the DNI be granted the authority to actually direct the IC by assigning missions, controlling the intelligence budget, and managing the personnel throughout the community, only then will there be a change from manager to director. In

36

order for this to happen the President of the United States must update the Executive

Order that governs the IC or Congress must draft a new law granting these new

authorities. As a result of the authorities of the DNI not being clearly defined, there

remains a very ambiguous relationship between all the leaders within the IC. In order to

overcome the limitations in authorities the DNI must possess and use interpersonal skill

in order to establish solid relationships with the leaders of each member of the IC.

Because the DNI is a political appointee, this means that the DNI position could change

every time a new President is elected. This turnover does not allow for continuity

amongst the community and can be a hindrance to effectively leading the IC. As a

political appointee, this also leaves the possibility that a non-career intelligence officer be

selected to lead the IC. As previously mentioned, relationships are crucial for a successful

DNI. The IRTPA of 2004 granted the DNI the authority to recommend people for the

position of Director of Central Intelligence. If the DNI is from outside the community,

this can lead to recommendations not based on merit but rather based on political support.

The IC cannot be constrained by politics and must be free to provide information based

on safeguarding national security. On the other hand, an individual who had spent his or

her career entirely in one agency might be equally biased for institutional rather than

political reasons.

Intelligence Centers

Another example of how the sharing of information amongst the members of the

IC has improved is the development of intelligence centers. The DNI, through the

direction of the IRTPA of 2004, created six intelligence centers that were formed to assist

the DNI and the IC to better share information amongst its members. While these centers have assisted the members of the community to gain information from each other in a more streamlined manner, there still remain some issues with the clearing of individuals from different organizations. Currently the IC does not have a common security clearance across the community. Due to a lack of standardization, individual members from amongst the community are not cleared to share in all aspects of intelligence. Different members of the IC process their clearances through different means. As a result of these clearances being processed by different means, there remains some doubt about the true validity of the clearance process. This leads to a lack of trust amongst community members and ultimately leads to the unwillingness to share information out of fear that information will be released and ultimately compromise a mission or worse, sources. If the DNI could direct that all members of the IC be cleared in a similar manner and standardize the clearance process, this would eliminate some of the lack of trust that develops between members of the community. Another solution to improve sharing would be a standardized database across the community. The need for compartmentalization will still remain; however, if all members of the IC are cleared in the same manner and allowed access to an IC wide standardized database, this will directly contribute to the DNI meeting the mission of improving intelligence sharing amongst the community. The "need to know" amongst the community needs to be limited to very special projects. In the interest of sharing information those members of the IC that are cleared and are given access to the database should then demonstrate, by the virtue of their job, that they in fact have a need to know the information stored in the database. The limiting of this information only serves to continue to hinder sharing amongst the members of the IC.

Addition of New Members to the
Intelligence Community

In order to effectively share information the IC added four new members to the community. Prior to the IRTPA of 2004, the IC had thirteen members under the control of the DCI. As the IRTPA of 2004 was implemented, the community grew to seventeen members now under the control of the DNI. The new members include the Office of the Director of National Intelligence, the Department of Homeland Security which is comprised of the U.S. Coast Guard Intelligence (CGI) and the Office of Intelligence and Analysis (I&A), and the Drug Enforcement Administration, Office of National Security Intelligence (DEA/ONSI).

The addition of these new members to the community clearly demonstrates the emphasis on securing the United States homeland from international or domestic terrorism. This addition also serves to unify all intelligence collection and analysis both in the United States and abroad.

Recommendations

Prior to conducting this research the author intended to find recommendations that would improve the community and the way intelligence is shared amongst its members. After completing the research the author was unable to establish recommendations that will completely resolve issues within the IC. However, the recommendations below will serve to enhance the way intelligence operations are conducted and can assist the DNI in his mission to increase intelligence integration throughout the IC. The recommendations will fall into three categories, "Standardization across the Intelligence Community,"

"Authorities for the Director of National Intelligence," "Further Research Recommendations."

Standardization across the Intelligence Community

It is the author's belief that the IC continues to limit its capabilities by not instituting and enforcing uniform standards across the community. This standardization should include security clearances, databases, and polygraph exams for all members.

Currently, among the seventeen members of the IC, security clearances are processed by more than one investigating organization. In order to begin to establish trust amongst the members of the community, the author proposes that all members of the IC be investigated to one standard.

There are more databases across the IC than the author could possibly count in an unclassified thesis. These databases, while holding very important information, lead to a duplication of information and an increased likelihood that information is not granted to those who require it. The author suggests standardizing databases across the IC and granting access to those members of the IC that are working in the specific area of interest. As with the first recommendation, this one also will serve to increase trust amongst members of the community while leading to an overall cultural change of keeping information from members outside the parent organization.

Building trust and confidence in the members of the community will directly lead to increased sharing and better team work. The IC is a team of seventeen members who, in order to be effective, need to trust one another. Trust is not established overnight and the author does not believe this is a solution that will have an immediate impact on the problem. However, the author recommends that all members of the IC, from the most junior person all the way to the DNI, should be subject to a polygraph that is consistent with current standards. Currently not all members are required to pass a counterintelligence polygraph exam. This exam will ensure a common process is applied to all members of the community thus working to build trust.

Authorities for the Director of National Intelligence

This research has shown that the current authorities for the DNI are inadequate. While the author is not implying that the DNI can't serve in his current role with the authorities that are stated in the IRTPA of 2004, the author does believe that the DNI is not a true director but rather a manager of the intelligence mission due to the limited authorities granted. In order for the DNI to effectively direct the IC, authorities need to be clearly stated in either a new law or an update to the Presidential Executive Order that grants authorities to the intelligence community. The author does not recommend a change to the structure of the IC but rather a clear law stating that the Central Intelligence Agency falls under the authority of the DNI and is not a completely-independent agency.

With the new authorities for the DNI, the author also believes that the new law or update to the Executive Order should clearly state that in order for a person to serve as the DNI he or she must have experience in the intelligence community prior to being nominated to serve in that role. As this is a political appointee, in theory the President of the United States can nominate anyone to serve in this very important role. This simple requirement will ensure that the DNI has the background knowledge that is required to serve the men and women of the IC as well as serve as the senior intelligence advisor to the President of the United States.

With these recommendations, the author suggests that congressional oversight be improved to ensure that the authorities of the DNI are granted and that the IC functions in a manner that is consistent with United States law.

Further Research Recommendations

While this research project attempted to identify the ways that the sharing of information has improved amongst the members of the IC since the IRTPA of 2004, the author did this in an unclassified manner. The author is unaware of any material that may be classified that could lead to different conclusions and recommendations but would suggest that the study be completed in a classified arena to ensure that all avenues are investigated. The author intentionally did not research any information from classified sources to prevent spillage into this thesis. This additional research may provide information that could lead to overall improvements in the functioning of the IC and for that reason, should be conducted.

The author did not research the details of the IRTPA of 2004 as it was originally submitted to the United States Congress. In conducting this research the author read articles detailing the limited authorities of the DNI but the author did not investigate if the authorities were in place when the draft law was first submitted to Congress and then subsequently removed for one reason or another. The author is not suggesting that authorities were stripped out of the IRTPA of 2004 but further research could prove otherwise.

This research did not include interviews with current senior members of the IC. The author recommends continuing this research by including interviews with select senior members of the community that may be able to provide some additional insight into the sharing of information within the community since the IRTPA of 2004. The author recommends interviews with the Director of National Intelligence, the Director of Central Intelligence Agency, and the Director of National Security Agency in order to gain their knowledge and opinions of how the community is operating and any potential improvements they might suggest. The author also suggests an interview with senior members of the Congressional Intelligence Oversight committee which may lead to answers regarding the authorities of the DNI as they exist currently and as they were initially proposed in IRTPA of 2004 before it was signed into law.

BIBLIOGRAPHY

Babington, Charles, and Walter Pincus. "Bush Vows Action on Intelligence Bill." *The Washington Post*, 1 December 2004.

Betts Jr., Richard A. IB10012, *Intelligence Issues for Congress*. Washington, DC: Congressional Research Service, 9 May 2006.

Burch, James. "The Domestic Intelligence Gap: Progress Since 9/11?" *Homeland Security Affair*. 2008. http://www.hsaj.org/?special:fullarticle=supplement.2.2 (accessed 20 March 2014).

Central Intelligence Agency. "Intelligence Community." www.fas.org/irp/cia/product/facttell/intcomm.htm (accessed 16 March 2014).

Collins, Senator Susan, and Senator Joseph Lieberman. Letter to White House Chief of Staff, Andrew H. Card, Jr. 10 June 2005. http://hsgac.senate.gov (accessed 29 March 2014).

Dozier, Kimberly. "Intelligence Director Dennis Blair Knew for Months His Days Were Numbered." *Associated Press*, 21 May 2010. http://www.csmonitor.com/layout/set/basic/From-the-news-wires/2010/0521/Intelligence-director-Dennis-Blair-knew-his-days-were-numbered (accessed 24 March 2014).

Eisenberg, Daniel. "Bush's New Intelligence Czar." *Time Magazine*, 20 February 2005.

Hardwood, Matthew. "Why Intelligence Reform has Failed." Security Management, 6 April 2010. http://securitymanagement.com (accessed 12 November 2013).

Hastedt, Glen. "9/11 Intelligence Reform: An Opportunity Lost." American Diplomacy Online, 27 October 2006. http://www.unc.edu/depts/diplomat/item/2006/1012/hast/hastedt_911intel.html (accessed 14 January 2014).

Hayden, Michael. "The State of the Craft: Is Intelligence Reform Working." *World Affairs Journal* (September/October 2010): 12-16.

History.com. "9/11 Attacks." http://www.history.com/topics/9-11-attacks (accessed 8 November 2013).

Intelligence Community Organizational Chart. http://www.intelligence.gov/mission/structure.html (accessed 16 March 2014).

Intelligence.gov. "A Complex Organization United Under a Single Goal: National Security." http://www.intelligence.gov/mission/structure.html (accessed 16 March 2014).

————. "Mission of the Intelligence Community." http://www.intelligence.gov/mission/ (accessed 15 January 2014).

Irwin, Sandra. "New intelligence Office Must Fix Information Breakdowns." *National Defense*, March 2003. http://www.nationaldefensemagazine.org/archive/2003/march/pages/new_intelligence3926.aspx (accessed 18 January 2014).

Jacques, Heinisha S. "Director of National Intelligence: Another Bureaucratic Layer or an Effective Officer?" Master's Thesis, U.S. Army Command and General Staff College, 2006.

Joint Chiefs of Staff. Joint Publication 2-0, *Joint Intelligence*. Washington, DC: Government Printing Office, 2007.

Kaplan, David E., and Kevin Whitelaw. "Remaking US Intelligence." *US News & World Report*, 20 December 2004.

Kibbe, Jennifer. "The Rise of the Shadow Warriors." *Foreign Affairs* 83, no. 2 (March/April 2004): 102-115.

Kindsvater, Larry C. "The Need to Reorganize the Intelligence Community A Senior Officer's Perspective." *Studies in Intelligence* 47, no. 1 (2003): 44.

Maguire, Edward. *Critical Intelligence Community Managing Challenges*. Washington, DC: Office of the Director of National Intelligence, 12 November 2008. http://www.fas.org/irp/news/2009/04/odni-ig-1108.pdf (accessed 22 January 2014).

McConnell, Mike. "Overhauling Intelligence." *Foreign Affairs* 86, no. 4 (July/August 2007): 49-58.

National Commission on Terrorist Attacks Upon the United States. *The 9/11 Commission Report: Final Report of the National Commission on Terrorist Attacks Upon the United States.* Washington, DC: GPO, 2004.

National Counterproliferation Center. Homepage. http://www.counterwmd.gov (accessed 17 March 2014).

National Counterterrorism Center. "Overview." http://www.nctc.gov/overview.html (accessed 17 March 2014).

Neary, Patrick C. "Intelligence Reform, 2001-2009: Requiescat in Pace?" *Studies in Intelligence* 54, no. 1 (March 2010): 1-16.

Office of the Director of National Intelligence. "Members of the Intelligence Community." http://www.dni.gov/index.php/intelligence-community/members-of-the-ic (accessed 19 March 2014).

———. "Mission." http://www.odni.gov/index.php/about/mission (accessed 21 March 2014).

———. "Organization." http://www.odni.gov/index.php/about/organization (accessed 21 March 2014).

Public Law 108-458. *Intelligence Reform and Terrorism Prevention Act of 2004*. Department of Justice, 17 December 2004. https://it.ojp.gov/default.aspx?area= privacy&page=1282#contentTop (accessed 4 November 2013).

Rettig, Michael. "Incomplete Intelligence Reform: Why the U.S. Intelligence Community Needs an Empowered ODNI." Diplomatic Courier, 12 February 2013. http://diplomaticcourier.com (accessed 10 November 2013).

Shorrock, Tim. "Revisiting Intelligence Reform." *Foreign Policy In Focus*, 6 December 2007. http://www.fpif.org/articles/revisiting_intelligence_reform (accessed 18 January 2014).

The 9/11 Commission Report. http://www.9-11commission.gov/report/911Report.pdf (accessed 10 December 2013).

The Robinson Library. "Clark Clifford." http://www.robinsonlibrary.com/america/ unitedstates/1961/biography/clifford-c.htm (accessed 21 March 2014).

Treverton, Gregory. Report 0-8330-3857-5, "The Next Steps in Reshaping Intelligence." Research Report, The RAND Corporation, December 2005. http://www.rand.org/ content/dam/rand/pubs/occasional_papers/2005/RAND_OP152.pdf (accessed 18 February 2014).

Turabian, Kate L. *A Manual for Writers of Term Papers, Theses, and Dissertations.* 7th ed. Revised by Wayne C. Booth, Gregory G. Colomb, Joseph M. Williams, and the University of Chicago Press Editorial Staff. Chicago: University of Chicago Press, 2007.

UNM National Security Studies Program. "The U.S. Intelligence Community." http://nssp.unm.edu/the-intelligence-community/index.html (accessed 16 March 2014).

U.S. House. Permanent Select Committee on Intelligence. *IC2I: The Intelligence Community in the 21st Century.* 104th Cong., 2nd Sess., 1996.

U.S. Senate. "U.S. Senate Select Committee on Intelligence." http://www.intelligence. senate.gov/churchcommittee.html (accessed 20 March 2014).

U.S. Senate Committee on Homeland Security and Governmental Affairs. "9-11 Commission, Homeland Security, and Intelligence Reform." http://www.hsgac.senate.gov/issues/9-11-commission (accessed 29 March 2014).

―――. "Testimony of Michael V. Hayden, U.S. Senate Committee on Homeland Security and Governmental Affairs." 12 May 2011. http://hsgac.senate.gov (accessed 29 March 2014).

―――. "Ten Years After 9-11: Is Intelligence Reform Working? Part I." 12 May 2011. http://www.hsgac.senate.gov/hearings/ten-years-after-9/11-is-intelligence-reform-working-part-i (accessed 29 March 2014).

―――. "Ten Years After 9-11: Is Intelligence Reform Working? Part II." 19 May 2011. http://www.hsgac.senate.gov/hearings/ten-years-after-9/11-is-intelligence-reform-working-part-ii (accessed 29 March 2014).

White House Chief of Staff, Andrew H. Card Jr. Reply to Letter from Senators Susan Collins and Joseph Lieberman, 21 June 2005. http://hsgac.senate.gov (accessed 29 March 2014).

White House. Executive Order 11905, *United States Foreign Intelligence Activities.* Federal Register, 18 February 1976. http://www.archives.gov/federal-register/executive-orders/ (accessed 18 March 2014).

―――. Executive Order 12036, *United States Intelligence Activities.* Federal Register, 24 January 1978. http://www.archives.gov/federal-register/executive-orders/ (accessed 18 March 2014).

―――. Executive Order 12333, *United States Intelligence Activities.* Federal Register, 4 December 1981. http://www.archives.gov/federal-register/executive-orders/ (accessed 18 March 2014).

―――. Executive Order 13355, *Strengthened Management of the Intelligence Community.* Federal Register, 27 August 2004. http://www.archives.gov/federal-register/executive-orders/ (accessed 18 March 2014).

Wilburn, William T. "The Under Secretary of Defense for Intelligence: Posturing Authorities to Complement Intelligence Community Reform." Master's Thesis, U.S. Army Command and General Staff College, 2011.